T0352670

LOT VEKEMANS

Lot Vekemans (born 1965) studied social geography at the University of Utrecht in the Netherlands and trained at the Schrijversvakschool 't Colofon in Amsterdam, graduating in 1993. Since 1995 she has written numerous plays.

In 2005 she received the prestigious Van der Vies Prijs for *Truckstop* and *Zus van*. Her play *Gif* (*Poison*) was awarded the 2010 Taalunie Toneelschrijfprijs for the best Dutch play staged that year.

In 2012 her first novel *Een bruidsjurk uit Warschau* (*A Bridal Gown from Warsaw*) was published and nominated for the 2012 Anton Wachterprijs for the best Dutch/Flemish debut. The novel has been translated into Norwegian and German. In 2016 she received Germany's Ludwig Müllheims Theaterpreis, the first time the prize has gone to a foreign playwright. Her plays have been translated into fifteen languages and have been staged successfully in more than twenty countries around the world.

RINA VERGANO

Rina Vergano is a leading translator of Dutch and Flemish plays, as well as poetry, libretti and films, and specialises in work for younger audiences and musical theatre. She has translated around seventy plays by leading Dutch and Flemish playwrights (many award-winning in their country of origin) for performance and publication. Rina is also a theatre journalist and playwright. Her new play *Horses! Horses!* will tour to Somerset pubs in the UK in 2018, co-produced by Wassail Theatre, The Theatre Orchard and Bristol Old Vic. She was a 2016 Leverhulme Scholar at The Egg children's theatre, who are co-producing her project *Harold* – inspired by the Bayeaux Tapestry – in collaboration with Le Vélo Théâtre and Bob Théâtre object-theatre companies from France.

Lot Vekemans

POISON

Translated by
Rina Vergano

NICK HERN BOOKS
London
www.nickhernbooks.co.uk

A Nick Hern Book

Poison first published in Great Britain in 2017 as a paperback original by
Nick Hern Books Limited, The Glasshouse, 49a Goldhawk Road, London
W12 8QP

Reprinted 2019

Gif copyright © Lot Vekemans 2010
Poison copyright © Rina Vergano 2017

Lot Vekemans and Rina Vergano has asserted their right to be identified
respectively as the author and translator of this work

Cover photograph © Shutterstock

Designed and typeset by Nick Hern Books, London
Printed in Great Britain by Mimeo Ltd, Huntingdon, Cambridgeshire PE29 6XX

A CIP catalogue record for this book is available from the British Library

ISBN 978 1 84842 710 5

CAUTION   All rights whatsoever in this play are strictly reserved. Requests
to reproduce the text in whole or in part should be addressed to the publisher.

Amateur Performing Rights   Applications for performance, including
readings and excerpts, in the English language throughout the world by
amateurs (including stock companies in the United States of America and
Canada) should be addressed to the Performing Rights Manager, Nick Hern
Books, The Glasshouse, 49a Goldhawk Road, London W12 8QP,
tel +44 (0)20 8749 4953, *email* rights@nickhernbooks.co.uk, except as
follows:

Australia: ORiGiN Theatrical, Level 1, 213 Clarence Street, Sydney NSW
2000, *tel* +61 (2) 8514 5201, *email* enquiries@originmusic.com.au, *web*
www.origintheatrical.com.au

New Zealand: Play Bureau, PO Box 9013, St Clair, Dunedin 9047,
tel (3) 455 9959, *email* info@playbureau.com

Professional Performing Rights   Applications for performance by professionals
in any medium and in any language throughout the world should be addressed
to Gustav Kiepenheuer Bühnenvertriebs-Gmbh of Schweinfurthstraße 60, D-14195
Berlin, Germany

No performance of any kind may be given unless a licence has been obtained.
Applications should be made before rehearsals begin. Publication of this play does
not necessarily indicate its availability for amateur performance.

The first performance of *Poison*, originally titled *Gif*, took place at NT Gent/NL on 8 December 2009.

SHE	Elsie de Brauw
HE	Steven Van Watermeulen
Director	Johan Simons
Designer	Leo de Nijs

Poison received its British premiere at the Orange Tree Theatre, Richmond, on 2 November 2017, with the following cast:

SHE	Claire Price
HE	Zubin Varla
Director	Paul Miller
Designer	Simon Daw
Lighting Designer	Mark Doubleday
Sound Designer and Composer	George Dennis
Costume Supervisor	Clio Alphas
Casting	Rebecca Murphy

Characters

HE
SHE

PART ONE

We see the chapel of a cemetery: an empty, white room containing a number of chairs. A water cooler and a coffee machine. HE is seated on a chair against the wall, a beaker of water in his hand. SHE enters, damp from the rain and a little chaotic.

SHE   You're early

        I saw your car standing there and I thought: he's early

HE   It didn't take as long as I thought

SHE   Shitty weather

HE   Yeah

SHE   Is the weather this shitty where you are too?

HE   Where we are?

SHE   In Normandy I mean

HE   Oh yeah, I mean, yeah yeah

        They look at each other.

        You haven't changed a bit

SHE   Oh, well don't look too closely

        HE *takes a letter out of his pocket and holds it up.*

HE   I only got it the day before yesterday

SHE   I didn't know if you'd get it in time

HE   I meant to phone you to say I was coming

        But em…

        I'm not much of a phoner

SHE   No, no, I've noticed

HE   But I'm here

SHE   Yes, you're here

Have you been here long?

HE   Twenty minutes

Half an hour, at most

SHE   Have you already been to his grave?

HE   It looks lovely

SHE   I do my best

HE   It's quiet here

SHE   It usually is in cemeteries

HE   Not many people I mean

SHE   Perhaps no one's died this week

HE   Sorry?

SHE   That's why it's so quiet

HE   Oh I see yeah

Well anyway they probably won't be burying any more people here will they

Considering the situation

SHE   No

No, probably not no

HE   Are we the only ones at this meeting?

SHE   They wanted to speak to everyone personally

HE   Okay

Don't you want to sit down?

SHE   In a minute

I've got bulbs in the car

Tulip bulbs

I wanted to plant them

HE   Now?

SHE   Yes or in a while

When it's less wet

HE   Right

So here we are then

SHE   Yes, here we are then

HE   I don't really know what to say

SHE   Neither do I

HE   You look good

SHE   Do you think so?

HE   Yes, I do

SHE   That's nice, nice of you to say so

Even though you probably don't mean it

HE   I do mean it

SHE   Then it's even nicer of you

…

You too

HE   What?

SHE   You look good too

HE   Thanks

SHE   France is doing you good, obviously

HE   Yes yes it probably is

Shall we sit down?

SHE   Fine

They sit down. First SHE. HE's *a bit unsure which seat to choose. Goes to sit next to her first of all, then reconsiders. Leaves a couple of chairs empty between them.*

HE   Nothing's changed here then

SHE   No

HE   Except that enormous hedge has gone I noticed

SHE   Too much upkeep

            Same with the rose bushes in the middle

            Someone's got to look after them and that all costs too much

HE   I thought it might have been the poison

SHE   No, no, it's got nothing to do with the poison

HE   Ridiculous eh

SHE   Dreadful

HE   And they've only just found out about it

SHE   They're talking about moving two hundred graves

HE   Two hundred!

SHE   It was in the newspaper

HE   So it *is* as bad as it said in the letter

SHE   Probably yes

HE   I thought it wasn't all that serious

            I mean, it said it wasn't a public-health risk

SHE   It's in the groundwater

            That's what it said didn't it?

HE   Yes, well, whatever, I expect we'll find out soon enough

            …

            Would you like a drink?

	Coffee, tea?
	Water?
SHE	No, thanks

HE gets up and walks to the coffee machine.

HE	Wow
SHE	What?
HE	They've got espresso, double espresso, cappuccino *and* latte
SHE	Yes, that's new

HE selects a coffee. Drinks some.

HE	Not bad
	Do you think they'll come and get us?
SHE	No idea

Long silence.

I'm finding this difficult

HE	Let's see what the options are first of all
SHE	No, I mean sitting here together, waiting
	Having to sit here… waiting
	And not having seen you for years
	And not having any idea how you are
	And you not having any idea how I am
	And not knowing what to say
	And absolutely bursting for a pee
HE	(*Laughs.*) You should just go to the loo then
SHE	Yeah, sorry

SHE goes. HE stays behind, hears a door opening somewhere.

HE   Hallo?

Is anyone there?

HE *goes and looks in the direction the sound came from. Knocks on a door.*

Is anyone there?

HE *tries the door, but it's locked.* HE *sits down again. His mobile phone rings.*

Oui

Oui c'était moi

Non, je suis arrivé

…

Non non ça va

…

Non, elle n'est pas ici maintenant

…

Dans la toilette

Oui, la toilette

…

J'ai aucune idée

Je te rappelle plus tard, bien?

…

Merci

Moi aussi

Oui

À plus tard

HE *turns off the mobile and puts it away.* SHE *comes in again.*

SHE   Pfff, that's a relief

        HE *smiles*. SHE *sits down*. *Short silence*.

        So, you don't think I've changed?

HE   Not really

SHE   Not at all?

HE   You've got older

SHE   Yeah what d'you expect

HE   I mean figuratively older

        Wiser

        Wise

        Wiser

SHE   Wiser?

HE   Yes

SHE   (*Laughs*.) If only

HE   I'm glad to see you

        On the way here I kept thinking:

        How will she look?

        How will she look now?

        And I couldn't stop thinking about the first time I ever saw you

SHE   That's twenty years ago

HE   I couldn't get it out of my head

        I hope you're glad to see me too

        HE *moves up closer to her*.

SHE   No don't touch me

HE   Sorry

SHE   Do you know what I find strange?

That things only happen when it doesn't matter any more

When you don't really need it any more

HE   Are you talking about me?

SHE   Partly

HE   So it doesn't really matter to you that I'm here

SHE   I'm not saying that

HE   You are saying that

SHE   But I didn't mean it like that

HE   You don't need me any more

SHE   No

That's positive isn't it?

If you don't need something any more

If you can do without it?

Not be dependent?

I mean it in a positive way

HE   So are you glad that I'm here or not?

SHE   I'm very glad you're here

That we're here now

Together

Washed ashore

So to speak

HE   Do you feel washed ashore?

SHE   Yeah well, no

In some way or other... yes

HE   In what way then?

SHE   Just

           Yeah

           Forget I said it

           It's more metaphorical

           SHE *gets up.*

HE   Where are you going

SHE   I'm going to go and see if I can find someone

           I mean

           It's nearly quarter past two

HE   I just heard a door

SHE   Where?

HE   Back there somewhere

           SHE *walks to the door that* HE *points out.*

           It's locked

           SHE *tries the door, knocks.*

SHE   Hallo?

           Is anyone there?

           Mr Alewijnse?

HE   Are you sure it was here?

SHE   That's what it said in the letter

           HE *takes the letter and checks it through.*

HE   Zuiderplantsoen 24-28

SHE   That's here

           Long silence.

           31st of December 1999

           It's a long time ago eh?

HE   Yes

SHE   31st of December 1999

HE   I know

SHE   At ten past seven

HE   You still know what time it was?

SHE   The door closed

I looked at the clock

Ten past seven

I can't help it

I'll just never forget it

HE   I'm sorry

SHE   What did you actually do that evening?

HE   I drove to Plombières

SHE   To your mother's holiday house?

HE   Yes

A bit before midnight I stopped in a car park just outside Nancy

I was the only car there

And I watched the sky above Nancy light up

There was only light

No sound

I thought that was so strange

That I didn't hear anything

That Nancy had entered the new millenium in silence, as far as I could hear

I felt

Yeah well actually, all sorts of things

I wanted to ring you, but then I thought: 'idiot, you can't just walk out on a day like today and then go and ring her at midnight'

So I didn't ring

SHE   I know

HE   It's funny actually

Well, funny…

I can't help noticing

More and more

How often you do things without really wanting to

SHE   Are you talking about that evening?

HE   No yeah, well yeah

I mean in general

For myself

That it's funny

How often I do things without really wanting to

And don't do what I actually want to do

That evening too, I think, yeah

SHE   You don't need to apologise

HE   I'm not

It's more of an insight that comes after the event

We probably all get to the same place in the end

SHE   Is that so?

HE   The same conclusion I mean

SHE   And what is that conclusion then?

According to you?

HE   That we do what we'd rather not do

And don't do what we'd rather do

SHE *laughs*.

That makes you laugh?

SHE Yes, to hear you say that

I think it's funny

HE Oh

SHE It is funny isn't it?

HE If you say so

SHE Are you getting touchy?

You're not going to start getting all touchy are you?

HE No

SHE But?

HE But nothing

Just...

Short silence.

SHE Don't you think it's bizarre seeing each other here after all these years?

HE *says nothing*.

I do

I think it's bizarre

Bizarre how things turn out

HE You could see it like that yes

SHE What would you call it then?

HE I haven't given it that much thought

SHE You haven't given it that much thought?

HE No, I haven't given it that much thought no

SHE You see me for the first time in ten years

HE Nine years

SHE   In this place

And you haven't given it that much thought

HE   No

SHE   Unbelievable

Is there anything you *have* given much thought?

Like what we're going to do if it is all true

If it turns out that those two hundred graves do need to be moved

What we're going to do then?

Where's he supposed to go?

HE   I want to hear what they've got to say first

What the options are

And the costs of course

SHE   The costs?

HE   There are bound to be costs

SHE   We're talking about Jacob's re-burial and you're talking about the costs!

HE   I'm sorry

I didn't mean it like that

Not how you just said it

SHE   How then?

HE   I just meant it in general

Please don't do this

You know I didn't mean it like that

It's ridiculous to act as if I meant it like that

SHE *goes to say something, thinks better of it. Long silence.*

SHE   I'm starving

HE   I've got a bit of chocolate somewhere

HE *fumbles about in his coat pockets, pulls out a bit of chocolate and gives it to her.*

You used to be addicted

SHE   Yeah

HE   Are you still?

SHE   Trying to cut down

Do you want some?

HE   I've already had three bars

Silence. SHE *eats chocolate.*

SHE   Did you know I got addicted to sleeping pills?

My doctor said it couldn't do any harm

That it was normal

For a woman in my situation

Because of everything I'd been through

Very normal, those sleeping pills

That's reassuring isn't it

I mean, that it won't get out of hand

The addiction.

No such luck

HE   Sorry, I didn't know

SHE   Do you know what the worst thing is about an addiction?

HE   How hard it is to break one?

SHE   How easy it is to develop one

It happens before you know it

You start off with a half

And then another half

Then a whole one

But not every night

Only if it's really necessary of course

And it is really necessary

So many things are increasingly really necessary

Things that come in pots

Or handy blister strips

And before you know it you're taking one every night

HE   That's the way it goes yes

SHE   For a long time I hoped that you could really put things behind you

HE   And then?

SHE   And then?

Start again of course

Yeah load of rubbish

It's never the same again

However hard you try

New job

New house

New friends

HE   It's never the same again

SHE   No

HE   Is that what you'd like?

SHE   Wouldn't you?

HE   To erase everything?

SHE   And start again, yes

HE   But where would you begin?

SHE   Where?

HE   Yeah, where would you begin?

        What day?

        What exact moment would you start erasing

        And how would you know that what came next would
        be any better?

SHE   That's a…

        That's a… stupid question

        SHE *fights back tears,* HE *walks over to her, embraces*
        her for the first time.

HE   Sorry, I didn't mean it that way

SHE   I miss him

        I don't miss him any less than I ever did

        Is that crazy?

HE   No

SHE   And you?

        Do you miss him?

HE   I think about him every day if that's what you mean

SHE   I mean do you still miss him

HE   I don't know what I'm supposed to miss

SHE   So you don't miss him?

HE   I'm resigned to it

SHE   That he's not here any more?

HE   That I miss him

        Every day

        Suffering's addictive, don't you think?

There should be rehab centres for it

With compulsory admission

SHE   Is that what you think?

HE   It sounds a bit weird maybe

SHE   Weird?

No, not that weird

More like... heartless

Maybe heartless isn't the right word either

More like... detached

As if it's not personal

I don't mean to you

More to the journalist

Your journalistic opinion yes

A male opinion as well

A male journalistic opinion about life

And suffering

HE   And what is this Male Journalistic Opinion then exactly?

SHE   The idea that you're in control of your own life

And in control of your own suffering too

HE   Don't you believe that then?

To a certain degree?

SHE   No, I don't believe it no

Do you think it makes any difference?

What you do or what you don't do?

Whether you're rewarded?

Or punished?

Or even worse: that it gets you anywhere to ask:

'what do I need to learn from this'

It makes me want to puke that question

'what do I need to learn from this'

Nothing

That life's shit

Sometimes

For some people

Really shit

For completely unexplainable reasons

HE I don't know if I agree with that

SHE Fine

 SHE *gets up and fetches a beaker of water. Downs it*
 and fills it again.

 Makes you thirsty

 Chocolate

 Tell me

 Why haven't you been in touch for ten years?

HE You want to know that NOW?

SHE Did you have another moment in mind?

 A better moment perhaps?

HE It's not something you can just

 That I can just…

 Here and now…

 You mean that I…

 Right here

Right now

I've got to explain…

SHE   You must have thought about it

HE   Yes

SHE   Or maybe you'd rather say why you left in the first place?

HE   You know very well why I left

SHE   Do I?

HE   Yes

SHE   A bit of explaining doesn't hurt you know

HE   And then?

If I explain, what then?

Or if I say I'm sorry?

Does it make any difference?

SHE   Sometimes it's nice to know you were right retrospectively

HE   Being sorry's not the same as being right

SHE   So, you've really given it a lot of thought eh

Sorry, I'm a bit fucked up

It's this whole mess here

HE   We could go outside for a bit

Go for a walk

SHE   In this weather?

HE   You used to like rain

Walking in the rain

SHE   Yes

HE   Well then

SHE   I'm not sure

HE   I'll go on my own then

        HE *is about to go.*

SHE   Don't…

HE   What?

SHE   No nothing

        I'll have another look and see if I can find someone

HE   I'll be right back

SHE   Yes, of course

        HE *goes.* SHE *stays behind, takes a drink and sits down.*

PART TWO

The same room. A bit later.

SHE *is sitting with a cup of water in her hand staring ahead.*
HE *comes in. Wet through from the rain.*

HE Do you know there's not one other car parked in the grounds

    That's weird isn't it

    Or does that Alewijnse cycle everywhere?

SHE No idea

HE You know him don't you?

SHE I know him by sight yes

HE Isn't there someone we could ring or something

SHE I haven't got a clue

    HE *takes out his mobile phone.*

    What are you doing?

HE Ringing that number in the letter

SHE Why

HE To ask why there's no one here

SHE There's no point

HE Why not?

SHE Because they probably won't answer

HE I can ring all the same

SHE We could just wait a bit longer

HE We've been waiting for over an hour!

SHE   So?

HE   It's almost quarter past three

We had an appointment at two

There's no sign of anyone

Anywhere

So it's not unreasonable to just ring then is it

SHE   I didn't know you were in such a hurry

HE   That's not the point is it

Maybe there's been a mix-up

Or maybe we're waiting in the wrong place

SHE   There isn't any other place here

HE   Why don't I just ring

SHE   Go ahead then

If you want to ring so much

But I'm telling you no one's going to answer

HE *dials the number in the letter. Waits.*

HE   Answerphone

SHE   I told you

HE *rings off and puts the phone away.*

HE   I think it's an odd situation

SHE   It is odd

HE   And d'you know what else I don't get?

Why the grounds haven't been fenced off

SHE   Not necessary I shouldn't think

HE   And why there aren't any warning notices up

SHE   Maybe they're going to put some up

HE   And the idea that he's been lying here for ten years
         already

         Ten years

         In that muck

SHE   Yes, that's terrible

         Terrible

HE   If you really think about it

         What that means

         If I try to imagine it

         Then then

SHE   You mustn't do that

         Really, you mustn't think about it

         Not like that

HE   No

         You're right

         You're totally right

         I mustn't think like that

         And in actual fact Jacob isn't lying there of course

SHE   Pardon?

HE   Well, in actual fact he's not lying there of course

SHE   In actual fact he's not lying there of course?

HE   No

SHE   If he's not lying there, who is lying there?

HE   I mean...

SHE   In actual fact Jacob isn't lying there of course

         You haven't changed a bit have you

In all those years

Not one bit

HE   I'm just trying to look at it in a different way

SHE   You're just trying to look at it in a different way?

Bullshit!

You're trying not to look at it at all

Just like always

HE   So, frontal attack

SHE   Just brush it off

HE   Would you rather I returned fire?

SHE   No

HE   Fine

SHE   I'd have to adjust my picture of you too much

HE *laughs*.

Yeah, amusing eh

HE   Did anything happen while I was gone?

SHE   Loads of stuff happened while you were gone

HE   While I was gone just now, I mean

SHE   Oh is that what you mean?

No

Nothing happened, just now

HE   Then why are you acting so differently all of a sudden?

SHE   I'm not acting differently

HE   You are, you're acting differently to when I arrived

SHE   Perhaps – on second thoughts – I'm not so glad to see you after all

HE   If that's the case then I'd better leave

SHE   Sounds familiar

HE   I'm not going to react to that

SHE   No I know

HE   Do you want me to stay?

         SHE *shrugs her shoulders*.

         You only have to say you want me to stay

         That's all

         SHE *says nothing*. HE *gets up*.

         I'm going then

SHE   Coward

HE   What did you say?

         SHE *says nothing*.

         You're not doing this

         No

         I'm not going to let you do all that... all your... your
         your

         I'm not up for it

         I'm not having it

         Really not

         HE *walks away*.

SHE   Sorry

HE   No

SHE   I said sorry

HE   No

SHE   Sorry sorry sorry sorry sorry sorry sorry sorry sorry

         Sorry

HE *stands still. Silence.* SHE *gets up and walks over to him. Stands close to him.* HE *doesn't react.* SHE *tries to catch his gaze but he keeps avoiding it.*

HE   What do you want?

SHE   What do I want?

HE   Yes, what do you want?

SHE *grabs hold of him rather roughly, as if she wants to lift him up,* HE *lets it happen.*

SHE   So, you've put on weight

SHE *tries to lift him up again, then pulls his jumper up.*

Ooh bit of a spare tyre there

HE   Don't

SHE   You're doing all right

Too many snacks is it?

A single man

They're not much good at looking after themselves

You should eat something healthy now and then
you know

And drink less of course

Doesn't anyone tell you that?

HE   Yes they do

SHE   Your mother I suppose

HE   My wife

SHE *is startled, walks away. Long silence.*

I had hoped that we

That we

Could make a new start

Today

I believe in it

In making new starts

Yeah…

Daft eh

SHE   Have you known her long?

HE   Two-and-a-half years

SHE   And all that time your mother's not said a word to me

HE   She didn't want to hurt you

SHE   Kind of her

Considerate

HE   It's not her fault…

SHE   No, of course not

…

I hate happiness

Happy people

Don't you?

HE *is silent for a while.*

They look so…

Never mind

HE   What do you see?

What do you see when you look at me?

SHE *laughs.*

I mean it

SHE *keeps laughing.*

You're laughing

Why?

SHE   I don't know

        Just

HE   You're laughing at me

SHE   No

HE   Does it feel better?

        Laughing?

        Laughing at me?

        Does it make you feel better?

SHE   Oh please, we're not going to start the deep
        psychological analysis are we.

        Woman laughs, but means: I don't know what to do,
        heeelp, I want to be serious but I can't do it

        SHE *laughs again*.

        Look sorry, I don't want to hurt you

HE   You're not hurting me

SHE   Good

HE   I'm just asking what you see when you look at me

        I mean it: What do you see when you look at me?

        WHAT do you see when you look at me?

SHE   I see eh...

HE   Be honest

SHE   I see a man

HE   A happy man?

        An unhappy man?

SHE   Stop this nonsense

HE   I mean it

SHE   What do you want me to say?

HE   What you SEE

SHE   I can't just look at you and say what I see

       I can't do it

       When I look at you…

       I only see…

       Flaws

HE   So you see a flawed man

SHE   No, it's not that you're…

       It's more…

       General

       Flawed, in general

       I see what isn't there

       And should have been

       I see a history

       A past

       A failed past

       Primarily that

       A failed past

       A failed story

HE   When you look at me you see a failed story

SHE   Yes

       It's true isn't it?

       You

       Me

       We're a failed story aren't we?

       I'm sorry, I can't see it any other way

HE   Did you know I was writing a book?

         Sorry

         I didn't mean to just spring it on you like that

SHE   A book?

HE   I probably shouldn't have said it at all

SHE   You're writing a book?

HE   Yes

SHE   What sort of book

HE   Just a book

SHE   A journalistic book?

HE   No, no

         It's prose

SHE   Prose?

HE   Yes

SHE   I didn't know you had aspirations

         In that direction

HE   It's a recent thing

SHE   Fiction then?

HE   Yes, well yes

         Partly

         Mainly in any case yes

         Silence.

         Don't you want to know what it's about?

SHE   No, I don't want to know what it's about no

         HE *goes over to her, goes to touch her, she avoids him.*

HE   It's about a man

         You could say that the man's me

Or partly me and partly the man whatever

It's about a man anyway

SHE   I don't want to know

HE   And about a boy

You could say the boy's him

SHE   I said: I don't want to know

HE   The man's suffering from…

SHE   What do you want me to do?

Do you want me to scream?

Do you want me to yell?

Throw myself down on the ground?

Or do you want me to throw glasses this time?

Is that what you want?

HE   I want to tell my story

My story

And I want…

SHE   Where did you get the idea?

I mean, where did you get the idea to write about something so…

HE   So what?

SHE   So… private

HE   Is that so strange?

SHE   I think it's… strange… yes

HE   The whole of world literature is full of it

SHE   Oh, so it's going to be world literature is it?

HE   I can understand you being cynical about it

SHE   I'm not cynical about it

I find it…

I don't know how to put this

HE   You find it too private?

SHE   I find it pathetic

HE   Pathetic?

You mean… dramatic?

Or pompous?

Sentimental perhaps?

SHE   I mean pathetic

I'm sorry… I don't have a better word for it

SHE *is silent for a while.*

Showcasing your grief

That's pathetic isn't it?

HE   I just want to give it a place

SHE   Give it a place

Why do we have to give everything in life… a place

As if it's a thing

HE   Close the book and put it in the cupboard

SHE   My life isn't a book that you can close

When I'm dead yes

Then maybe, maybe then yes

HE   You'd rather *be* your grief?

SHE   Yeah, yeah, maybe I would yeah

Maybe that's preferable to… to…

Giving it away to whoever

Just because they happen to pay fifteen euros for it

If you're lucky

Short silence.

HE   I don't expect you to be happy that I'm writing a book

SHE   Good

HE   But in some ways I'm writing it... for you too

SHE   For me?

HE   For us actually

SHE   For us?

HE   Yes

SHE   Just tell me

What is that... 'us'... then?

In your eyes

What are we, us two together, then?

HE   We're...

A man and a woman

Who've lost a child

Who first lost a child

And then... each other

Or perhaps I should say:

Who first lost a child, then themselves and then each other

SHE   That's a

Very

Clear

And concise

Summary, yes, of us

SHE *starts to cry.*

HE   If you can only feel grief when you think of
      someone…

      When you think of someone you've loved…

      So… incredibly much

      And if nothing new comes to take the place of that grief

      Then aren't you doing something very… wrong?

SHE   I AM full of grief

      That's my right

HE   Is it?

SHE   I've lost a child

      We've lost a child

      Then you have a right to grief

      I think you have a right to grief then

HE   And imagine that you still had a child?

SHE   I haven't got one

HE   But imagine

      Would he have the right to a grieving mother?

      Or a grieving father?

SHE   I'm not in the mood for your hypotheses

HE   It isn't a hypothesis

SHE   Do you remember when someone said we should just
      have another one?

      Another one!

      As if they were talking about a cat

HE   Perhaps we should have done

SHE   You don't mean that?

HE   I do mean it

SHE   So you *would* have… [liked another child]

HE   Why not?

Does it get any better if you don't go on

No

Does it get any better if you do go on

Maybe not

But it's worth a try

SHE   (*Is silent, looks at him for a long time in astonishment, almost shock.*)

You're a father?!

Aren't you?

You're the father of another child?

HE   Does it make any difference?

SHE   Are you the father of another child?

HE   (*Emphatically.*) WHAT DIFFERENCE DOES IT MAKE?

SHE   Is that why you've come here?

To tell me that?

HE   I came here because you asked me to

SHE   I wanted you to come here, because I thought…

Because I hoped…

HE   That I'd be just as hopeless as you are?

Two drowning people clutching the same lifebuoy?

SHE   Is it a boy or a girl?

HE   I haven't got a child

Not yet

SHE   Not yet?

HE   Valérie is pregnant

SHE   Valérie?

HE   That's her name

SHE   Valérie?

HE   Yes

SHE   She's called Valérie

HE   Yes

SHE   And Valérie is pregnant?

HE   Yes

SHE   By you?

HE   Yes!

         Look I'm sorry to spring this on you

         The whole thing

SHE   How old is she?

HE   Valérie?

SHE   Who else?

HE   Does it matter?

SHE   Young of course

         Young, fresh, optimistic

         And beautiful

         I bet your mother's mad about her

HE   God you're so bitter

SHE   Oh and why would that be?

HE   You think you're the only one in pain eh

         The only one who has pain and grief

         Your drama

Everything was always your drama

From day one

Your son

Your loss

Your suffering

As if I had nothing, nothing at all to do with it

And why?

Why?

SHE   You didn't see him being run over

You weren't even there when it happened

HE   Oh no, not that again

I wasn't there when it happened

No, I wasn't there when it happened

I was at the office writing up some crappy article about fuck-knows-what

I know yes

I didn't SEE it happen

But I felt it

I felt it very clearly

Here

HE *hits his body*.

And here

And here

And here

Everywhere

Everywhere yes

Long silence.

When I first got to Plombières I went running a lot

I ran for kilometres

Up and down hills

Through woods

Alongside fields

To deaden the pain

That terrible pain

In my stomach, in my chest

And with every kilometre I ran, I got further away

From everything

More deadened

More lost yes

I had no idea where I was

Or what kind of weather it was

I just put one foot in front of the other and kept going

SHE   But luckily at the end of the journey a beautiful young French woman was waiting for you and she opened her arms and took you to her beautiful French house where there was a fire glowing in the hearth and yes, then you knew you'd come home. And after years and years of running you were finally where you needed to be. At home, with Valérie...

HE   Don't do this

SHE   And before you knew it your beautiful young French wife was pregnant...

HE   Don't, I said

SHE   And then suddenly you thought: hang on, I used to have a son somewhere in Holland, years ago, who was tragically run over by a motorist who was tearing along a street at eighty kilometres an hour. Oh yes, it

was sad, but happily life goes on. And somewhere
inside that grey brain a brilliant idea hatched: I know,
I'll write a book about it.

HE   DON'T DO THIS

SHE   A book, yes, about me and my son and how difficult it
all was, even if you had to dig really deep into your
memory, because you could hardly remember how it
had all gone actually...

HE   Stop it, please

SHE   But perhaps I, your pathetic ex-wife, can help you a bit
with the details, because as far as I'm concerned it's
never ended, you know, never. Every moment, every
detail, everything, everything, everything is recorded
in this head, perfectly preserved, like in a 3D film.

HE   STOP

       NOW

SHE   Don't touch me

       SHE *pushes him away hard and in doing so, catches
       him in the face. His nose starts to bleed.*

HE   Ow

       Shit

       It's bleeding

       HE *searches for something to staunch the bleeding and
       at the same time tries to hold his head backwards.*

       Have you got a hanky or something?

       SHE *looks in her bag or jacket. The only thing she can
       find is a hairband or something similar.*

SHE   Here take this

       HE *takes it and dabs at his nose, meanwhile:*

HE   I understand that you're angry

SHE   Oh yeah?

HE   You're angry because I left

SHE   Really?

HE   You feel as if I deserted you

SHE   Feel as if?

HE   Yes

SHE   You did desert me

Didn't you

That's not a feeling

That's a fact

HE   I left

With two suitcases

On New Year's Eve

The day before the new millenium

At ten past seven

That's a fact

SHE   Gosh yes, let's get *all* the facts straight then shall we

Do you remember what I was wearing?

And what the weather was like?

HE   You were wearing jeans and a red tracktop

SHE   Well remembered

No really

Very well remembered

I underestimated it, that memory of yours

Memory for detail

I'd almost say: a real writer's memory

HE   Do you want me to offer my apologies?

SHE   Do you want to?

HE   I've already said I'm sorry

SHE   That's nice yes

       Noble

       Magnanimous

       You're sorry

HE   And you

       Are you sorry?

       SHE *laughs in amazement.*

       Well?

SHE   What do you mean, am I sorry?

HE   You didn't do anything

SHE   Exactly, I didn't do anything

HE   That's what I mean

SHE   What do you mean, exactly?

HE   I mean that you didn't do anything

       What I said

       That's exactly what I mean

       Very simple me

       No hidden agenda

       No dot dot dot and fill the rest in yourself

       I said: you didn't do anything

       And that's exactly what I mean

       You just let me go

       With two suitcases in my hand

On New Year's Eve

You didn't block my way

You didn't come after me

Bravo!

Well done!

You didn't do anything

SHE *is shocked*.

SHE   It's just unbelievable the way you twist things round

HE   Oh yeah

SHE   Still

HE   I think it's unbelievable the way you still wallow in your grief

SHE   Oh yeah

HE   Like it's a lovely warm bath

SHE   You really don't know what you're talking about

HE   No of course not

SHE   Not a word from you in ten years

HE   Nine years

SHE   And then…

HE   Then what?

SHE   Then this

HE   Then what?

SHE   This…

These…

I haven't got any words for it

HE   I had hoped that things had changed

That you had changed

SHE   And you then?

HE   I've changed

        I've changed a lot

SHE   Me too

        In some ways

HE   Oh yeah?

SHE   Yes

        I've come to terms with what happened to me –
        sorry, us

        I'm not saying I've accepted it

        Or that I understand it

        No

        But I've come to terms with the fact that this is my life

HE   And that's it?

SHE   I do things, okay

        I've got a job

        I've got friends

        I do sport

        All very normal

        Like a normal life I mean

        I get up

        I have breakfast

        I

        I have coffee with the neighbours

        I read the papers

        I know what's happening in the world

        Who's starting a war where

I can have conversations about things

At work

At a birthday party

Or a street party or whatever

Yeah

I join in

I join in yeah

That's all you can expect of me

HE   And that's how you're going to go on for the next
        thirty, forty years?

SHE   What's wrong with that?

HE   Everything

SHE   You think you know it all better eh?

HE   I'm not saying that

SHE   But?

HE   I don't understand you

SHE   Why do you want to understand me so much?

HE   You're my ex-wife

        We've got a history together that will never disappear

        Whatever we do

        I want to put a full stop after it

        Put a full stop after it, together

SHE   Put a full stop after it?

HE   Yes

SHE   You're really good at metaphor aren't you?

        No, I mean it

        So consistent too

Full stops, sentences, stories, books

I can really see that you're a writer nowadays

Crazy really

I thought that being a writer was something you had in you your whole life

Something you couldn't avoid

I never knew you could still discover you were a writer after your fortieth

Reassuring actually

That everything's still possible

That even I could still BE something

And still discover it

Exciting

HE *gets up*.

What are you doing?

HE   I'm going

SHE   Maybe you could come up with something else for a change, other than going

HE   There's no point

        I'm sorry

        I can't do this any more

SHE   I'm glad you've said it

HE   I really had hoped it would be different this time

        That it was possible

        That you and me

        Something different

        Well anyway

        It's not different

SHE   And that's all my fault of course?

HE   No

      I don't know

      It doesn't matter

      It's just not working

      I don't understand you

      You don't understand me

      And apparently that's still the most important thing in
      our lives

      That we understand each other

      So if that doesn't work

      Then that's that

      I'm sorry but I think it's best if I go

      HE *walks away, stops, hesitates.*

      There's just one thing I'd really like to say

SHE   And that is?

HE   That when I was driving here…

      I kept getting an image of the first time I ever saw you

      Twenty years ago

      And I noticed

      That when you smiled

      You got a little dimple

      Just here

      On the right side of your cheek

      And I'd just forgotten

      I'd just forgotten that you had that

And you can believe me or not, but I was really happy
that I'd got that image back again

And I just wanted to tell you

That I was happy that I'd got that image back of you
when you smile

HE *goes*. SHE *remains behind, alone*.

PART THREE

In the same place. Much later. SHE *is still sitting there.*

HE *comes in with a bottle of wine and a large piece of French cheese.*

SHE	You're still here
HE	Yes
	The car wouldn't start
	I mean: the car would start, but I couldn't start it, I mean, I couldn't do it
SHE	Oh
HE	I saw someone closing the gates
SHE	Alewijnse?
HE	Yes
SHE	Did you speak to him?
HE	Yes
	And I rang home
	To say I'd be here for a bit longer
SHE	Good
HE	I've got some cheese
	If you fancy some
	And wine
	I brought it with me for my mother
	Do you want some?
SHE	Okay

HE *puts the things down and opens the bottle, pours, meanwhile:*

HE   Friendly man, that Alewijnse

SHE   Yes

HE   He lost his wife last year

SHE   Oh, I didn't know that

HE   Breast cancer

SHE   Oh

HE   He said that they're going to expand it here

          On the west side

          And that they're going to clear some old graves

          From the early 1900s

          The families kicked up a big fuss

          It was even in the papers

          He'd had sleepless nights over it he said

          He didn't know who I was, but when I mentioned Jacob...

          I told him that I live in France now

          He didn't really react

          He told me to give you his very best wishes

          He said it twice

          'Give her my very best wishes'

          SHE *says nothing, drinks wine.*

SHE   Nice wine

HE   He said he'd leave the gate open a bit longer

SHE   That's kind of him

HE   He gave me a number to ring when we want to leave

          Then he'll come and lock it

HE *cuts a piece of cheese and gives it to her.* SHE *eats it.*

SHE   Nice cheese

HE   Are you cold?

SHE *nods.*

Why don't we go somewhere else

Somewhere warmer

SHE *shakes her head.* HE *takes off his coat, puts it round her shoulders*

SHE   You hate me don't you?

HE   No

SHE   If you don't hate me, what then?

HE   You want to hear me say I love you

You want to hear me say I still love you

And then you'll say: I don't know

SHE   Is that what I'm like?

HE   That's what you're like

SHE   I don't want to be like that

HE   I know

Short silence.

SHE   My brother's just bought a house in Portugal

A quinta

That's what he calls it

Two hours drive from Coimbra

And do you know why?

HE   Because he can afford it

SHE   Because he loves Portugal so much

He absolutely loves Portugal

He says

He's actually in love with it

Really in love

He says

He can feel it in his body

Physically feel it

My brother loves Portugal the way other people love their dog

I'm not making it up

He really said that:

'I love Portugal the way other people love their dog'

Portugal is like a… pet… to him

I don't understand that

I… don't… understand… that

How can you love a patch of soil

As if it has a heart

As if it needs you

That's so…

Short silence.

HE   You used to love people-watching in the train

SHE   Is that so?

HE   Yes, that is so

And reading out loud from the letters page in the newspaper

SHE   Was that all I loved?

People-watching in the train and reading out loud…

HE   From the letters page in the newspaper yes

SHE   Ridiculous

HE   And you loved pinwheels

              And gobstoppers

SHE   As a child yes

HE   Not just as a child

              And you loved people who got tears in their eyes while
              they were talking

              And sheets that hadn't been washed for at least two
              weeks

              And you loved peonies

              Butterfly bushes

              And wine with dessert

              And Sting of course

              'Fields of Gold'

              How many times have I heard that song

SHE   Sometimes I get the feeling that my head is so full

              Of all sorts of things

              That I...

HE   Can't forget

SHE   Mustn't forget

HE   I remember the exact way we drove to the hospital

              The whole way

              Exactly

              And arriving in the car park

              And walking to the entrance

              Through the sliding doors

Into the entrance hall

That looked like a shopping centre

With a gift shop

And a flower stall

And a new restaurant with wooden chairs and tables dotted with big bright-blue plant pots

We said to each other that in a week's time we'd be sitting there eating an ice cream with him

Or pancakes

And those squeaky footsteps on the linoleum in the corridors

And those vast lifts

SHE   I'm tired of it

HE   What?

SHE   With every step I take he's with me in my head

Filling the kettle for tea

Opening the fridge and shutting it again

Buttering bread

Slicing cheese

Pouring milk

He's there everywhere

HE   Sometimes I see a man

An ordinary man

With a boy on the back of his bike

The man points: look a dog, a cat, a pigeon

The boy smiles

Or a man teaching a boy to swim in the lake

The boy's scared and cries, the man shouts, slaps the surface of the water: you can do it! come on, you can do it!

And I keep asking myself

Am I that man?

Is he that boy?

Which snapshot are we?

SHE I don't want it any more

HE I know

SHE If it's always going to be like this

Then what's the point of going on?

HE Do you remember me asking you:

Can you believe that things like this happen for a reason?

You looked at me as if I was mad

There's no sense in things like this

No sense and no reason

Things like this just happen

Randomly

That was your truth

But your truth kept dragging me down

Into a deep whirling vortex

That got deeper and deeper

Till I couldn't breathe any more

SHE I'm sorry

That I'm like that

HE I don't want you to say that

SHE   But it's how it is

        Sometimes I see people who have been through far
        worse

        And who can deal with it

        I hear them say they're happy

        I can see them being happy

        And then I ask myself:

        What's wrong with me?

        What am I doing wrong?

        And just that thought alone makes me feel…

        And that's the way it goes on

        And on and on

        Do you understand?

        HE *nods*.

        Why did you go?

        Why that evening?

HE   I couldn't do it

        Counting down the minutes till midnight

        Raising a glass

        Cheers

        Making a wish

        A new year

        I just couldn't do it

        Looking at you

        Hugging

SHE   I remember the soft click of the door closing

        Just like that

As if you were going to work

Or popping out for some shopping

As if you'd be right back

And then the car starting up

I counted

Thirty seconds before you drove off

Thirty seconds to change your mind

I kept on counting

Fifteen seconds

Till the sound of the car disappeared

Blotted out by the sounds of the street

The fireworks

The neighbours

The thumping of my heart

I looked at the clock

Ten minutes past seven

It's right yes

It's right what you said

I didn't do anything

I didn't try to stop you

I let you go

With two suitcases in your hand

On New Year's Eve

HE   You have no idea how hard it was to drive away

At every corner I thought:

Go back

At every traffic light I thought:

Go back

Go back

But I couldn't

SHE   I stood in front of the window all evening

With the lights out

And I kept thinking about the last moments with Jacob

At the hospital

You on one side of his bed

Me on the other

Someone saying: we're going to disconnect him now

How long

How long do we have?

A couple of minutes?

A quarter of an hour?

At the most

And I heard myself thinking:

This isn't the time to cry

I held him tight

For the first time in weeks I held him tight

Without tubes coming out of his body

Without the sucking sound of the respirator

The peeping of the heart monitor

Just him and me

Two bodies against each other

I could feel his chest rising and falling

His fingers in mine

Warm blood

Beating blood

The world stood still

In some way or other it was a complete moment

Completely whole

Me

And him

Nine minutes

In the end it turned out to be nine minutes

HE   I was glad it was over as well

Over for him

It's crazy how you start to hope that someone will die

Give up

Let go

Go on

Just go

It's okay

We'll manage

We'll manage without you

How wrong can you be

SHE   Yes, how wrong can you be

HE   Don't you think it's strange that we're here now
talking about this for the first time?

SHE   It was just like everything in my head closed down

HE   That made me angry

SHE   I know

HE   There were so many times I felt like hitting you

Just so you'd feel something again

Me

Your husband

The father of your child

SHE   I know I know I know I know…

HE   I was so scared that I'd actually do it you know

Hit you

SHE   Is that why you left?

HE   Partly yes

Why don't we go somewhere else

SHE   And then?

HE   Carry on talking to each other somewhere

Maybe we could eat something

SHE   I don't feel like having people around me

HE   We could go to your house if you like

SHE   To mine?

HE   Why not?

If you'd prefer it

SHE   No, not to my house

HE   What do you want then?

SHE   I want to stay here

Like this

Like now

HE   And then?

SHE   I don't know

        I want you to say that everything will be all right

        That everything will be all right in the end

HE   Everything will be all right

SHE   Oh yeah?

HE   Yes

SHE   When?

HE   One day

        At a certain moment

SHE   One day yeah

        On my deathbed probably

        HE *laughs*.

        Do you think that's funny?

HE   Yes

        On your deathbed yes

        That'll be just in the nick of time then

        HE *laughs louder and it gets her laughing too. When they stop laughing, it's silent for a moment.*

        Where did you get the idea for the letter?

SHE   What?

HE   This letter

        Where did you get the idea of writing it?

SHE   There was a thing in the paper about old graves being cleared

        A big hoo-ha about it

HE   And that poison?

SHE   That was at the old gas factory

        They were on the same page, the two things

The graves and the toxic ground

Yeah, I know you think I'm mad

HE   I don't

SHE   I am anyway

HE   Why don't you go and talk to someone?

I know you never wanted to, but…

SHE   Do you think I've never seen anyone?

I've seen all sorts over the years

Psychologists, counsellors, psychotherapists

And the only thing they said was:

Yes, it is heavy

Yes, it is a lot

Yes, it is difficult

Yes, it will never be the same again

HE   What were you expecting then?

SHE   I want to be happy again

Is that too much to ask?

HE   No, of course not

SHE   I want someone to save me

HE   It doesn't work like that

SHE   No?

HE   No

SHE   It's easy for you to talk

You've been saved

HE   How's that?

SHE   A new woman

And soon, a new child

HE   It's not like that

SHE   Oh no?

HE   Do you want to know what saved me?

SHE   Yes of course

HE   I took up singing

SHE *laughs*.

I knew you'd laugh

SHE   Sorry, I didn't mean to

SHE *laughs again*.

Oh sorry, really

Don't tell me you've joined a church choir

HE   It's a men's choir

Don't laugh

SHE   No, I think it's great that you've started singing

Really

I like the idea of you singing in a men's choir

A French men's choir

HE   I turned up really early one day

We rehearse at a school

In the gym

I was standing outside in the playground waiting for the others to arrive

And while I was standing there I suddenly heard someone singing

In the gym

With a very deep voice

One that can reverberate through walls

He was singing something in English

Which is strange, because usually we sing in French

It was 'It Must Be So'

By Bernstein

D'you know it?

SHE *shakes her head.*

I didn't know it then either

But it was beautiful

It was so incredibly beautiful

That very deep voice

I could feel every note vibrating through my body

Like I was singing it myself

It felt just the way your body feels when you're singing yourself

Like that

And I suddenly thought:

What if everything stayed exactly as it is now?

What if this is it?

And it was just like everything relaxed because of that thought

Do you know what I mean?

SHE   No

HE   What if we didn't get any further than today in our lives

Than this moment

That nothing bigger, nothing better, nothing more beautiful comes along

That this is it

SHE   Sounds terrible to me

HE   Does it?

SHE   Yeah

HE   Really?

SHE   That this is it?

HE   Yes

SHE   That nothing better comes along and this is it?

HE   Nothing better, nothing more beautiful

SHE   Terrible

HE   But it would be a relief too wouldn't it?

        Not to need anything else

        Not to expect anything else

SHE   But that's ridiculous

HE   Why?

SHE   Being happy because there's nothing else

        Because you don't have to expect anything else

HE   It's peaceful though isn't it

SHE   But not very hopeful

HE   What would you prefer?

        Hope or peace?

SHE   That's oversimplifying it

HE   You'd rather have it complicated?

SHE   So you stood in that playground

HE   Yes

SHE   And you heard that man sing

HE   Yes

SHE   And you thought: what if everything stayed as it is now

HE   Yes

SHE   And then?

HE   It made me feel relaxed

        Or at peace

        And then I mean really at peace

        And it was just… good

        Look it's really hard to explain

SHE   Maybe you should sing that song

HE   It's not about the song

        It's about the effect it had on me

        What happened inside me

SHE   Maybe then I'd understand it

        Wouldn't I?

HE   The point is that in one instant I could see everything differently

        Experience everything differently

SHE   I don't believe in that

HE   It's not a question of belief.

SHE   What is it then?

HE   It happened

SHE   Just like that?

HE   Yes

SHE   Because of that man singing 'Let It Be So'?

HE   It must be so

SHE   It must be so

HE   Yes

SHE   I hate that

Those stories

HE   What stories?

SHE   Those sort of stories

Stories that just happen to some people

That aren't logical

That you can't reproduce yourself

It makes it all so...

So...

HE   So what?

SHE   So intangible

As if you have to see the light first

Only no one tells you how to do that bit

HE   See the light?

Do you think I've seen the light?

SHE   Sounds like you have

HE   It's more like being a bird who's discovered how to fly

SHE   I feel more like a bird who doesn't know that it can fly

And who has to leave the nest

HE   That sounds like you don't have faith in anything
any more

SHE   Nope, I don't have a shred of faith

That it will all be all right in the end

Or that I will ever be happy again

Really happy, I mean, like before

HE   Perhaps you shouldn't want to be

SHE   Happy?

HE   Like before I mean

           Perhaps we should stop wanting it to be like it was before

           Perhaps we only have to accept that it is

           And that it's all right

SHE   And then be happy with life I suppose

HE   Yes

SHE   And is that what happened with that singing?

           Were you happy to be alive?

HE   Yes, I think so yes

SHE   That's nice

           Do you sing a lot?

HE   Every week

           Every Tuesday evening

SHE   In that men's choir

HE   Yes

           And you?

SHE   Do I sing?

HE   Yes

SHE   Never

           Yeah, at birthdays

           (*Sings quickly.*) Happy birthday to you, happy birthday to you, happy birthday dear hmm-hmm, happy birthday to you

           That's about my level

HE   You sung to Jacob

SHE   When he was a baby yes

HE   And in the hospital

SHE   Did I sing in the hospital?

HE   Don't you remember?

SHE   No

HE   Just before he died

          I was holding you

          And you were holding him

          You sung very softly

          With your lips pressed against his forehead

          I couldn't really hear what it was

          Don't you remember?

          SHE *shakes her head*.

          I've often wondered what it was you sung

SHE   Are you sure I did?

HE   Competely sure

          SHE *gets up suddenly*.

          What is it?

SHE   I want to get out of here

HE   Now?

SHE   Now yes

HE   Now immediately

SHE   Now immediately yes

HE   Is it because of what I just said?

SHE   No

          Yes

          As well

          I don't know

It's because of everything

All that

Today

HE   And then?

SHE   I just want to leave this place

I need to go

HE   Do you want to go somewhere else?

SHE   I want to go home

HE   Do you want me to go with you?

SHE   No

HE   What then?

SHE   Nothing

I just want to go home

Alone

HE   We can't just leave each other like this

SHE   I'm sorry

Really

Really

You have to believe me

I'm really sorry

HE   I don't want you to leave like this

SHE   It's okay

HE   It's not okay at all

SHE   It's okay for now

It's okay for me

HE   Is there anything I can do for you?

SHE   No

I can't think what

Nothing probably

HE   Can't I do anything at all for you?

Now

This moment

SHE   Maybe hold me

HE *walks to her and holds her.* HE *presses his lips to her forehead and softly sings 'It Must Be So'.*

HE   My world is lost now
And all I loved is dead
So let me trust now
In what my master said
There is a sweetness in every woe
It must be so
It must be so

…

Are you laughing?

SHE   It's beautiful

You singing that

HE   I'm not a great singer

Not like that man

SHE   It's lovely

Really

I think it's lovely

Thank you

HE   I want to go with you

Home

To your house I mean

SHE   I don't want you to

HE   We can't leave each other like this

SHE   Maybe we have to accept that this is it

        Just like you said

HE   I'm finding it difficult to leave like this

SHE   It's fine

        I mean, it's not fine, but it's how it is

        I live here

        You live there

        You've got a new wife

        You're going to be a father soon

        And I really hope everything goes well for you

HE   What about you?

SHE   I'll probably become an old spinster with warts on my
        chin and a hairy nose

        Joke

        Joke!

HE   Maybe you'd like to come to Normandy some time?

SHE   No

        But I would like to hear from you now and then

HE   Me too

SHE   Will you drive home carefully?

HE   I'm going to my mother's first

SHE   Okay

HE   So this is it?

SHE   Yes, this is it

HE   That's the best we could do?

SHE   Yes, it's the best we could do

          It's the best I could do

HE   Right, then I'll go and ring Alewijnse

          HE *takes his phone and a piece of paper out of his pocket.*

SHE   Alewijnse?

HE   I promised

          That I'd call him when we were leaving

SHE   I would have forgotten

HE   (*Rings.*)

          Mr Alewijnse?

          …

          I promised I'd ring you when we were leaving

          …

          No we're going now

          …

          Fine

          Very nice of you to let us stay

          …

          Yes, you too

          …

          I'll do that yes

          Bye

          HE *rings off and puts the phone away*

          All the very best from Alewijnse

SHE   Again?

That's the third time today

HE   Some people are always friendly

SHE   Some people are yes

They leave.

End.

www.nickhernbooks.co.uk

facebook.com/nickhernbooks

twitter.com/nickhernbooks